AMERICAN
PRODIGAL

AMERICAN PRODIGAL

POEMS BY

LIAM RECTOR

STORY LINE PRESS

This publication was made possible thanks in part to the generous support of the
Nicholas Roerich Museum, the Andrew W. Mellon Foundation, the National
Endowment for the Arts, and our individual contributors.

Thanks also to Virginia Sandy and the staff at Agni.

The cover is Edvard Munch's "The Sick Child," courtesy of the Epstein Family
Collection. The book is designed by Tree Swenson.

Library of Congress Cataloging-in-Publication Data
Rector, Liam, 1949–
        American Prodigal / Liam Rector
            p.   cm.
        ISBN 0-934257-21-3 (cloth); 0-934257-22-1 (paper)

Story Line Press, Inc., Three Oaks Farm, Brownsville, Oregon 97327-9718

Acknowledgments

Some of the poems in this book appeared, sometimes in different versions, in the following magazines:

Agni: The Night the Lightning Bugs Lit Last in the Field Then Went Their
    Way, Working Wrong in the Late Republican Eighties, Your Early Livid Days
American Poetry Review: Him, His Place; My Business Partner; Three Portraits
    of Boy
Boston Phoenix: Association
Boulevard: Elizabeth Bishop, Summer by the Water, The Widows
Harvard Magazine: Age Moves
The New Republic: Hans Reading, Hans Smoking; The Remarkable
    Objectivity of Your Old Friends
Paris Review: Getting Over Cookie
Ploughshares: Our Own Ones, Uncle Snort, We Should Not Let Munich
    Slip Away
Poetry East: Devoid of Ornament or Rhetoric of Any Kind
The Reaper: Old Coat
Virginia Quarterly Review: Tonight We Bow
Western Humanities Review: My Pony

The author would like to thank the editors of these magazines for their work.

"The Night the Lightning Bugs Lit Last in the Field Then Went Their Way"
also appeared in *The Best American Poetry 1992*, (Scribners/Collier), edited by
Charles Simic and David Lehman.

"Him, His Place" is for Donald Hall, "My Business Partner" is for Donald
Justice and Jerry Winestone, and "Working Wrong in the Late Republican
Eighties" is for Michael Lehman and Askold Melnyczuk.

Thanks to friends for their kinship and critical reading of the manuscript. This
book is further dedicated to the filmmakers Rainer Werner Fassbinder (1945 –
1982) and John Cassavetes (1929–1989); to the teacher Rudd Fleming (1908 –
1991), and to Polly Fleming. Thanks also to David Rector.

As well, the author would like to thank the John Simon Guggenheim Founda-
tion for a fellowship in poetry, which buoyed matters.

For Virginia Rector

& for Tree Swenson

TABLE OF CONTENTS

The Out of the Woods Monologues

The Meathouse Monologues

The Tidewater Monologues

THE OUT OF THE WOODS MONOLOGUES

The young placed their bets on the flesh, knowing they were to lose.

Albert Camus

THE NIGHT THE LIGHTNING BUGS LIT LAST IN THE FIELD THEN WENT THEIR WAY

We went out into the field to get away from the others, to make
Love, and there they were—hundreds of them—lighting their last night
In the shudder, the quickening cold, the shifting weather come then

To gather them in…Towards what? Anything there for us, after?
Already hundreds had gone down but surely this was the last night
Even for the strongest among them, and as the cold entered us we went

Quickly down. First you on top of me, then with your legs wrapped
Around me and me pushing as deeply as I could, going into you, as if
There were some great depth I would not be having the time to go into.

HIM, HIS PLACE

My grandfather died one morning in dampness,
Tamping, watering the roses for the coming season.
On his knees then, he must have bowed

To the worn harness snapping in his chest and sending him
Finally into memory for us, into the waters of spirit
Submerged and afloat From Then On. He must have known before

—He said nothing about it—that he would soon be going
From us. People look back and say that the dead, days
Before they die, have their ways of saying goodbye to us,

If we only knew what to look for: he did visit
Relatives he'd long ignored and went
To sing his agnostic prayer in their church,

The week before he left us; and he went so far
As to ask my grandmother, a woman he had not slept with
For twenty years, to fix his favorite meal for him,

The evening before he died. And she went ahead
And fixed it. Part of what you got as a tenant farmer
In those days was the morning milk, two pigs a year,

A cinderblock house, and a plot where you planted
What your family needed—but I think what kept him alive,
Aside from the habit of living, was the evening

And the hills he watched each evening after eating,
As some people watch water. Those were the staring hours
In which I came to know him, sitting with him, watching

The fields move and all but live our lives for us.
As the cows shifted and the cars moved by below at the bottom
Of one field, I felt the motion of field the man carried

So eloquently with him. And when I asked him
About women, as I did often that last summer
I came, he usually said nothing—though as a sparrow

Mounted a sparrow one evening he did mention
A woman from a time long before mine, remembering outloud
"The stiff cock I gave her in the back of a buckboard,"

Buckboards driven out to drive-in movies just before
The horses went back to the field, just as the farms
Were giving themselves over to the trucks, the tractors . . .

I howled in complicity, thinking I was getting, at last,
Some real man-talk from him. It was the cars
Eventually took all his children from him, the ones

After the war which the children jumped in
And used to drive towards the money, the cities,
The places where I grew up on the movies.

I lived in the suburbs and was eighteen, between things,
When told over a phone he would no longer
Be there to sit with. I had been the only one

He finally ever talked to, and I thought of him, his place,
As the only home I ever had. . . . Decades later,
After my generation's war and the stalling we did

Having children, my second wife and I had our first child,
Virginia, and filled our rowhouse near the water of Baltimore
With the sound of two oars placed in the water and drifting...

And tonight, as I was moving inside Mary with a stiff cock
Ruddered towards our second child, we both went down into
      those fields
Moving between us, and heard there the sleep of children as they move

In the wet darkness of their first home before it perishes
And they dry-dock into the body of boat and the fate
Of water, the great collapsible moment of motion we are.

OUR OWN ONES

I will be coming up the hill from school in an hour....

Lena stretches to the clothesline as Carl
Is coming slowly back over from the barn....
Between them the field dips deep and the field

Slopes long and half the day, already, is done.
She pushes a wooden pin onto a cotton skirt
And the wind competes for dominance here.

He'll live until his sixties; Lena into her nineties....
The fields will reside when they're gone
And the farm, as farms do when the property is not

Owned, will change hands, change families.
I will make a living somewhere else
Making lines I remember from the life

I saw here, using forms from what held us
While in the hold of this place, but for now
I will be coming up the hill from school in an hour....

My mother got caught and put
In the penitentiary. My father
Could not afford me or did not

Want me (both struck me
As true) so I was sent out
To the country while he worked

A failing business in the city.
In the 1950s, after the war,
People from the country,

Along with people from other
Countries, made their way to
The American cities. The food

Was still grown in the country
(Where else could it be grown—
On roofs in the cities?),

But the real hurl of action turned
Towards the marketing of things
In the major American cities.

Suburbs, full of people
Who did not know how to live
In them, soon formed

Around the cities, and I swore
I would do something
About this, someday, but the day

My mother was sent up I got
A break from this mess for a moment—
I was sent out to live with them,

With Carl and Lena in the country.

Carl moves towards the lunch of pork which Lena
Has left on the table. He will eat, crap, sit while
He's able, and be back over to the barn in an hour.

Lena will come in, feed herself, phone on the party line
The woman down the hill, and they will wade
Through their loneliness as late afternoon goes over.

I will be coming up the hill from school in an hour.

    Built cheap, built to sell quickly, thrown up
    To house men back from the killing, women
    Going back to the home from the factories

    Where they had worked to support The War Effort,
    And children about to be born and form the single
    Largest generation in American time, the boomers,

    The suburbs in the post-war era were built around
    The car: carports, forts isolating each family,
    Each adolescence for the children spent without

    Any real place to gather other than the mall,
    The market, or the woods (and adolescence is
    Nothing if not a strenuous effort to come in

    Out of the woods), and meanwhile in the cities
    The old houses torn down to put up housing
    'Projects' for the poor: hanging schizophrenia

    In mid-air, bad buildings, wrong turnings,
    And much of it dynamited down by the 1980s ...
    Just before those my age took the helm in the 1990s.

They were kind to me. They were glad to have me.
At first they thought they were too old, really,
To tend to me, but I tried to be a good boy for them

—I spent much of my time alone in the woods anyway—
And soon they were glad to have me. I would fetch
Things for them and unlike their other ones, gone

To the city, I was enchanted by the country;
I didn't yet have to make any money.
I was their grandson come to live with them then

Late in their lives with their children raised
And the love all but gone from their marriage.
They took me in and they loved me then

And without them there would have been no rudder....
I got older, they died, the farm got sold out from under
Everyone, and again I took on the fate of the cities.

With Carl and Lena gone that was pretty much the end
Of any of us getting together as an extended family.
The American family changed, and though many tried to

Will the old family back (such will is cruel;
Such cruelty expressed itself politically),
Most took up forming the different family.

I now have a daughter, I'm divorced, and I make a living
As an architect in Cincinnati—forming windows, arcs, lanes...
And though I know there's no going back I try to bring back

Something of the nineteenth century town to the American city.

AGE MOVES

Age moves in the hound
As it was in me moving
Through forest I found

As to dog I went
That year scrounging
Through Manhattan....

The wood opened out,
Unlikely in the city,
As to boy slandering

To leave his fitful home,
Bright he might survive
With his pen-knife only.

THREE PORTRAITS OF BOY

1

When I was a boy a boy when I was a boy
I thought the language was a language
Would send me everywhere there was to go.

I thought there was something to know
And I took off with a mind full of language
And a need to get away from what I took

To be the stupidity around me. I took off
Early and I went far and I never looked back,
Except I kept hearing the old songs, kept singing

The old hymns, and they're all I hear now
Since I landed for a moment in this hospital
In this college town....Now when I hear

Harbor, when I hear *harness,* when I hear *harden*
Or *Harvard,* they all mean the same place where
I am lost and without moment, without even

The holy and silly ignorance of choir in my ears.
In the hospital which was kind enough to take me
I have spent violent hours hallucinating, constructing

Homes I can go back to—which are not homes anyone
Can go to—but only way-stations for all that breaks down.
I think it was hate sent me here, hate I could not stop

Hating, contempt for a world which would not stop
Turning and would never get any smarter
Than the stupid thing it was. And the doctors

Tell me I will have to turn this hate somewhere, into
Something, if I ever hope to see the outside of this place
Again—if I ever hope, somehow, to ever start over.

2

To begin again nothing again
But the lunging and the going
On down into the staring—

The inert, entropic, looking-to-be-
Alive-again clearing
Where we wait in the field to hear

And hear there again in our minding
The old life calling,
Which forms then the new life....

Too much rouge not letting the decay across,
The choir deep in its pleading and bragging,
Too righteous with too much Christ hanging high

On the horror cross, and so boy leaves
The country church, gravel upended
On the long road it takes getting out,

And boy leaves the small town in favor
Of Baltimore and all that comes
To a port town staring out its own window

By the water as a city sails towards and away
From itself, singing in its sailing
What those who journey need most to hear.

Whether we suddenly go or habitually wait
As drinkers do in the Irish bar by the water
In the afternoon, or take up the smaller action

Of standing and thinking by Poe's grave,
The port city offers the same freedom we look for
In the first drink—port cities drinking themselves

To death singing   If we stay too long
                     It will be the the same song
                     And we will be less

                     For having stayed to sing it.

3

Every evening after I get something to eat
I take my machine and go down smaller and smaller
Roads until I am completely

Lost on the back roads, tongue-tied and baffled
By all that shoves hard, as it all does,
And listening to my country on the radio,

To the psycho, to the sounds of going that never
Stop whining, wailing, caught in the rigging.
I can't say no to the compass that points me down

The back roads, into the spine and nape where
The dust glows, alongside the gape and the curve
Where the river knows, and on to the turn

Where I don't know. My brother, who left here
Early, was at Harvard taking his *orals* when he had
His breakdown...He was a guy who liked looking for things,

It appeared to me, but he could have been just running,
Just trying to get away from the same things
I get away from, or to the side of, by driving my machine.

When we were young and he first left I took it
That he didn't like us, didn't like the life here
With us, couldn't stand to stay here like us,

And went away to spite us...We were the two boys
Who could talk to each other early, before any way
Of acting, any way of speaking in public came to us,

And whether it was *Pass the salt* or *Help me,*
We had our ways of staying with each other.
So when he wrote from college about his breakdown,

When he wrote to say he had *gone down,* I first
Offered to go there but then he told me to *stay put*
Until he made his way back to where he came from.

MY BUSINESS PARTNER

You who have eaten so often
And with such deliberate pleasure: wheat
Weeping with the cutting at the end
Of the napping and yellow summer,
Fat vegetables waving
Goodbye, goodbye to the vine,
Whole cows stunned at the slaughterhouse
Divided in their end from each other
And the mother sun under which they grazed.
You are forty and paying for things now

And have been for some time....
You are no longer the boy lying in the field
In Virginia feeling the keel of coming fall,
Mulling over what moved through you last night
At the drive-in movie, refusing to budge
Because you know this will be your last summer
Before jobs, newspapers, empire, the entire world
And worry of being one of the boys
In America, in the Manhattan through which
We now food-hunt, many lying

On the feral bottom in boom town, our town,
Like so many downed and eaten ones we came upon
In the early forest....Today we make our return
In exhaustion from the work world to the wide open
Where we were once boys, fooling; today
Our daughters lie in the same field laughing
Over what fools we are; today we look over
To our wives, wonderful—not the harpies we feared
Looking at the '50s in America, the Don't-Tell-
Daddy, the family sequestered then in each house,

Each shadow, before the entire damned thing flew apart.
The Soaring Divorce Rate is something
We visited early, our sins—and the one
It comes down to, indifference—forgiven between
Us and our wives then....The family extended,
In necessity, to take in even "the broken home" now....
This is the place where your father spent
His last summer on earth last summer, your mother
Still grieving but proud at least we have not spent
Most of our lives in prison so far, given

Who we are, given how much trouble in mind we gave her
Coming up—our business doing almost well now....
And it rattles down to this: the business
Of any nation is business, as the great bore said.
We had hoped for something other (To be taken
Care of? Complete, cleansing destruction?),
But it fell to us to practice an ongoing circulation
Of art and money: hunger followed
By production followed by distribution
Followed by hunger—the hunger,

The hunt, the eat. Everywhere, and I hate
To see it, people are ground up not having
Gotten to their production, but the distribution
Goes on because it has to, because it remains
What we have between us? We fight to get
To our real work, and ours has been to cover,
With the documenting image, what we never got over
In that field, in what moved before us up there
On that screen at that drive-in. So we make movies
To make money so we can make more movies and an audience,

In repose, has seen what moved through us that summer....
Back in college, where we were both dreaming like monks
Of the world outside and the world to come,
Most of our teachers taught us business was vulgar.
But they were hiding from the hunt and they are
Making their money explaining to the young
Our movies now....I think it is tragic
And hilarious, what's become of us,
Having grown towards so much of what we hated
Just as surely as we grew towards what we loved.

The body begins the work of coming out from under us
Just as the field was always busy, we knew, devouring us.
Meanwhile my wife teaches retarded children to ice-skate
And your wife makes a killing in medical research;
You are buying your first house and your testicles
Tighten at the expense, and I am slowly building back
After having flown apart one more time....What keeps
Most people from remaining criminals is turning
Thirty-five? At forty, as one of the good teachers
Said, men *learn to close softly the doors to rooms*

They will not be coming back to, and no matter
How mortgaged the house is, for our renting moment
On earth, our daughters—taking in *le cinéma* indoors—
Are now having their summers before they go
About the business of somehow finding their work.

THE MEATHOUSE MONOLOGUES

Condemned to drift or else be kept from drifting.

Bob Dylan

OLD COAT

Dressed in an old coat I lumber
Down a street in the East Village, time itself

Whistling up my ass and looking to punish me
For all the undone business I have walked away from,

And I think I might have stayed
In that last tower by the ocean,

The one I built with my hands and furnished
Using funds which came to me at nightfall, in a windfall. . . .

Just ahead of me, under the telephone wires
On this long lane of troubles, I notice a gathering

Of viciously insane criminals I'll have to pass
Getting to the end of this long block in eternity.

There's nothing between us. Good
I look so dangerous in this coat.

There's the dish outside the window, filled with rain.

—Tom Waits

I put in my hours here every day
So I can have what I have at home:
A clean, sequestered place
Where I can be alone.
I have my weekends plus holidays.
I cooperate with my co-workers
Not because I like them especially
But because I know how interconnected
All our duties are and how much trouble
Any of them could make for me
At any time, should they take a mind to.
If there *is* trouble we meet
And do what we can to *iron out* the trouble,
Though those of us who have been here for any time
Know this never works for us,
So we find other ways.
My efficiency apartment is much
Like the office: clean and lots of light.
The streets are a mess so I don't
Go out much. When I do go out
It's usually to White Flint Mall
Or to one of my favorite restaurants.
I have a car, which I trade in
Every three years so it stays nice.
I can afford it. Because I've stayed
So long at the job I'm earning
The good money now.
I also have a bicycle, for my health.

I sit so much at my job my health
Slips away, if I don't watch it.
I have to keep an eye on myself.
My brother, cross-addicted to alcohol
And to drugs of every description,
Is a messy person with a messy life.
My sister still goes from job to job.
My parents say that when they die
They will give me the house we all grew up in
Because I'm the only one
Who knows how to *appreciate*
That kind of thing. I want peace.
I don't want drama of any kind.
My brother says he's acting out the logic
Of his deepest feelings, demons and all,
And I can see what kind of mess that is.
He says he is also a mirror
Held up to our wild and disruptive times
And then he laughs his lewd and sardonic laugh,
Which is just a lot of *sarcasm* to me.
I have a nice boyfriend I've gone with now
For over four years. He has trouble
Committing himself but I don't let that
Bother me too much. He's nervous.
I think someday I can do better so I let him
Stay as uncommitted as he likes . . .
My sister says she won't settle
For the vapid *or* for the horrified
Life I lead. She tries to stick it to me
And says there's not much life
Left in me . . .
And she's always saying there's *got*
To be *more*, more! But she wants drama
And I can see very clearly

The mess she's setting in motion.
We're all over thirty-five now. We have no children
And my brother says that's bitter.
And the way I figure,
Who would know better
About what's bitter?
And my sister's taken to saying
We should all locate our future
Somewhere closer to the water,
As if that mattered.

UNCLE SNORT

My aunt was upset by lesbians:
Her sister, her sister's lover, in particular.
She imagined them, I think, giving each other

Head over and over, though from what I knew
—And I knew plenty—that couple made love
With roughly the same frequency

As did Auntie and Uncle Snort. They
All had plenty to worry about, though since
The minds of the Snorts were bent

Around projecting their demons wildly
Onto others, introspection—and the following
Quiet and responsibility comes there—was lost

On the Snorts, which worked out pretty well
For them most of the time, except theirs were
Unexamined Lives, stupid beyond belief,

And they were hell to pay come election-time.

We used to visit each other often back when
You were painting (alone you thought) The Big
Picture.... "I depend entirely on color.

I explain nothing, and I depend upon the rapacious others
To chat up my labor." I used to come over
To witness your desire to be taken, to be hung,

To draw in the money and the rumor, without, actually,
A moment's effort. "If I don't feel like it I don't
Do it. Maybe one a month. Sometimes paint

Straight from the can and sometimes broken glass."
Your feeling was for the American, the American
Scene, for which you got down and acted as vessel.

"The rent overtook me. I left for the country."
Our scene was in fact the hysterical, the hysterical
Desire under things, for which we acted as vassal.

We did right by your death and went out,
Right away, to a public place to drink,
To be with each other, to face it.

We called other friends—the ones
Your mother hadn't called—and told them
What you had decided, and some said

What you did was right; it was the thing
You wanted and we'd just have to live
With that, that your life had been one

Long misery and they could see why you
Had chosen that, no matter what any of us
Thought about it, and anyway, one said,

Most of us abandoned each other a long
Time ago and we'd have to face that
If we had any hope of getting it right.

DRAMA PRODIGAL

Peace? So you want
Peace now? You're
Tired of the drama

And want to come in,
Want to have a little
Place of your own,

A little piece of the action
For yourself now? Isn't it
A bit late? Couldn't you

Have called first? I'm not
At all sure things can be
Put right at this

Late date ... But
Come in. Anything
I can get you? Any way

We might talk straight
Like we used to?
Your bed, if you must know,

Is still there, but I'm not
Sure, not sure at all
You should stay here.

If I do take you in
And you don't *stick*
This time ... If you

Run back to the drama
The way you ran
All the other times

Those of us who love you
Held out the healing hand
Of love to you … If you

Run off again like that
There'll be
No peace on earth

For you, no
Getting away or
Stepping aside

From the hole we'll
Make for you, and you can be
Damned sure I'll hold

You to that.

PROPERTY

From place to place with no one place
To lay the head, to tether
And so gather and find repose from

The adventure of getting through the weather
And each other....What was it—
Some kind of real estate swindle in Eden

Gave some people places and others nothing?
Do we inherit it, earn it, or is it mine
Based only on my ability to take and defend it?

ASSOCIATION

Odd looking fuckers, thousands of us gather
At the Hilton in winter, to promenade and scratch
Among each other. At least five thousand

Here looking for jobs, and god knows why
The others ... Are they getting honoraria?
Waiting for some country to finally come in

And take us, our theme this year is The
Victims of Other Cultures. Positions for all of us
This year at Harvard? Not this year ...

Ever? On the video at the bar Michael Jackson
Says he is looking at the man in the mirror
And asking that man to change his ways.

I not-so-secretly love video, and so do the others.
Fifty jobs here this year so next year fifty
Of us can stay home and not have to go out

And walk through the valley of each other.
This is what we imagined when we got going
On all this: life of the mind; off summers.

THE WIDOWS

Here are the hotels and the widows
And the windows out of which
The widows stare towards the water.

Out there, they know, in the movement
Of what feels like nothing but keeps moving,
Are the spirits of their men gone off.

So many gone off and so many women
Left staring, in a final gathering of women.
And here I have returned this fall,

Having breezed in off the mainland
To pick up some quick cash
Serving the widows. They know

I have come here again to retire from love
In the off-season, having found no one
To abide with, in my travels.... And as

I serve them their biscuits and coffee
In the morning, they are sad to see me back
But they joke with me: Will I never

Settle down? Will I ever start a family?
And when I lie down with one in the afternoon
She tells me she loves the smell

Comes off me, no matter how much a boy
I am, and I do not tell her how frightening
Her own scent is, how near and damp

The grave seems each time I'm in her.
I learned early to love the fallen breasts
Of the mothers, sucking and giving back

Something they'd lost with their husbands,
But these widows are now past all that. . . .
I know an analyst would say I'm lying

With my mother—I'm no doubt lying about
Something—but I mean to exhaust the entire time
Before I stop, before I stay, before I come in

To start a family or to make another widow.

FOUR OLD MEN

Four old men, childhood time
  More real to them than time now
    And certainly time of their twenties, forties,

Sixties.... That time glimpsed only,
  When glimpsed, as decades spending
    —Providing, along with their wives, for their children. . . .

Four old men, farts almost ready
  To let go now ... One saying, "I dug deep enough
    So the hole turned into the fort, the place to go I needed."

"She took off her clothes
  And so did I and by god I showed her
    What exactly it was I had." "They ground me so fast,

So badly into that playground dirt,
  They turned me into most of who I am, even now."
    "The first part was lonely. I hadn't yet met Mary."

GETTING OVER COOKIE: A MADE-FOR-TV-MOVIE

In the ninth grade I met a fantastic number of times
With Cookie Harris in the woods....Under the pretense
Of going over our Algebra notes, given the pressure
Of the pop quizzes being served up then
With an alarming frequency, we'd have at
Each other, kissing and squishing against
Each other....She'd stop, in a manner
Peculiar to those times, once I had my first full feel
Of her breasts (enormous and soft, as I remember,
A source of fascination and grief
To every frenzied boy I knew),
And then we'd go into the dry-humping
Segment of our routine until one of us
Rolled over and it would all be over....
We would return, sitting on the invariably damp ground
And in utter depression, to the formulas
And to the grade-gettings of the day....
She wanted me to be her boyfriend and led me
To believe I could go farther, much farther,
Should I but make the noises of consent
On that front, but I had eyes
For one of the DiFilippo twins
Who lived across the tracks and resented me
For the poverty of my parents and my acne
(Which Cookie had a touch of as well—
We were poor kids on the outs, with only
Bad skin to inherit), so with an eye cocked
Towards Cheryl DiFilippo I withheld what was then
The violent tumult of my callow affections. . . .
This kind of Marxist melodrama, rife
With all its underpinnings of dominance
And submission, haunted me well

Into my twenty-fifth year when I met and married,
In a veritable dither, one Alison Cromwither,
In a ceremony covered by the *New York Times*
Which took place at the estate of her approving parents.
Alison's father was a bull-boy broker and her mother
Was left-leaning and as cultural as they came
In those days....Between them
They sponsored a fine literary press which issued
Its four slender volumes each year, and as it happened
My own debut in verse was soon among those in
The next batch to appear....The book became known,
Befamed immediately for the surge and pith by which
It dismantled the hidden injuries of class in America,
And her father was soon convinced I was just the fellow
To restore the meanness and the juices he was certain
Bryn Mawr had taken out of his increasingly anorexic Alison.
Far from snubbing me owing to my humble origins,
Bull-Boy saw in me the stirrings of his own early anger
And hysteria, and trusted that fire-in-the-belly intensity
To lift Alison suddenly into the bounties of nature
And make for the bellowings which had in the past attended
His own breakthrough, business successes....
He told me it seemed as though I had just come in
Out of the forest....And I could see that the mother,
Whatever her misgivings, could hardly wait
To get her affluent mitts on me, to lie down with another
Of "her" authors....Alison made an ideology
Out of everything in those days, a habit of mind
I took to be remarkably transcendent and high-minded
Until it became clear, altogether too clear,
That this was part of an irrefutable (and not political)
Sorrow and anger eating at her, all the while
Saddening and outraging her, blurring, in effect, whatever accuracy
Her thinking might otherwise have held. . . . As alluring as she was,
She was always perilously close to being committed,
Never far from the mental ward of it all.

And given how confused and co-opted I was, after my efforts
To administer to Alison and urge her, with not a whit of luck,
To place herself in the hands of an expensive professional,
I took to cavorting in the kick-ass bars of my beginnings,
Looking to recapture there some semblance of a wilder world
Still in the lurid process of getting-ahead
Or looking to forget that discreet stampede
Within the waters of yet another squat and guzzle....
When I was soused I felt like a boy again,
And all I could think of was Cookie, Cookie.
Even when hungover and having to face myself in the morning,
Gratefully handsome after the crater-faced rigors of my adolescence,
All I could see through the clearing was Cookie's face....
What began as the python thirst of pleasure soon turned
Into the worm of need and habit and I was spirited off
To a clinic myself, where Bull-Boy assured me
It was all part of the game and urged me forward again,
Back into the ring. His wife was off to a spa,
Longing for weight loss, and he desperately needed someone
In whom he could confide....Things went on this way well
Into my thirties, by which time I was chairperson
Of many philanthropic organizations (so many pigs,
So few troughs; so many sluts, so few slots),
And I continued to write savage,
If irony-crippled, verses, until one day
Alison announced she would be gone
For the weekend, sequestering herself, as had become
Her debilitating gesture, in our cottage on Nantucket
By the incessant ocean, where she would undoubtedly
Sit by her "grieving window" and run her bony fingers
Up and down the chill of the pane, while moaning....
Rather than accompany her, I decided to jump
Into our Alfa Romeo, given to us recently
By Alison's mother and used by Mummy and me for our sordid trysts
In the surrounding countryside, and I floored it
For the Middle Atlantic section of the country,

From whence I had so long ago come...and there she *was,*
Perched in the same squalid neighborhood, getting by
In a mean but well-kempt hovel, and with a dignity
Well beyond her years....Cookie was there, ineluctably
There, as were tales of abortion, betrayal
Tales of lugging impossible tracts by Trotsky
Off to her job as a receptionist, to be read
When her boss wasn't looking or promising her a raise
If he could but once stare upon the naked flesh
Of her "jugs" revealed (and she all the while trying
To delineate through her reading what historical forces
Had brought her to this abyss of desolation). Her autodidact obsessions
Moved me beyond all belief, and I was on the phone to New York
Immediately: I would not be coming back. I would be
Staying here with Cookie....Bull-Boy, older now and damaged
Beyond redemption himself, saw this for what it was—
My *last chance,* and one he might well have given himself
Had he but the foresight, the opportunity, or the still-burning-fire.
He vowed to notify Alison as soon as he could penetrate her
Solitary vigil on the Cape, and said were she not answering
He would leave a message for the idiot on her desperate tape....
And he said to go ahead and keep the car!
I could not then, nor as things came to pass
Did I ever, abandon my romantic Tory sense of reality,
But coupled with Cookie's Commie zeal I was certain
We could make a go of things, and for many years
We did....We looked out for each other,
Laid down fully in the firm grip of each other,
And though we were too soon swallowed
In the deeper forests to come,
My sole measure of triumph and loss rises and falls
Around those final years with Cookie before she left me driving
An aging sports car without her
With too much, finally, to ever get over.

THE TIDEWATER MONOLOGUES

We acquire the habit of living before we acquire the habit of thinking.

Albert Camus

SUMMER BY THE WATER

You left, took our daughter,
And by the time the two of you returned
I was living in another city

By the water, having talked my way
Into the job, into the money I could not locate
Before you left and took our daughter.

(Forgive me. I could not put things over.)
You visit me here now with her after all our
Quarrels over the distance, over the wires,

And you and I are happily not able
To keep our hands off each other....
Out of work a year ago, last summer,

I was convinced we were a nation
About to go under. I saw us as a country
Always going off to invent again—specializing

In putting asunder—a motion having trouble
Placing one foot in front of the other.
And now we're together and surrounded again

By so much water and our betrayal—bow
That our daughter is again convinced
We want her—where will we go with all

We've come to doubt of each other?

FIRST GRADE

Allen Newport, famous in the first...Allen, forever
Fixed in the first for me unless I see him, unlikely,
Ever again....Allen getting his butt kicked

At recess; at lunch one day two assholes hocking
Into Allen's bologna on white, two saucy boys
Unable to stop messing with cross-eyed, dazed

Allen, and lord how I did enjoy beating the living
Shit out of one of them later, at my leisure,
In the courtyard where we really got to know each other

In that grade, that era, that site of spitting and so much
Defeat rising out of a sandwich, that first of many schools
I went to getting to know Allen and the people like him,

The ones who come up to you when you first get somewhere.

TONIGHT WE BOW

Not to worry about writing too much
Copy, being too busy, or lacklove
In what strikes us as winning ugly

In the late 1980s....Children now,
More life to be paid for: Virginia
Moving tonight some turns she learned

In the first grade, all of us turning
Still in the first grade, dancing tonight
The seven love songs of Hawaii, lovely

Absurd twistings we move with now after
Exhaustion, exhaustion come over us
Like that other emotion, worry over money.

I hated you in my twenties. I thought you
Prissy, clipped, without range or ambition...
Precise—I always gave you that—but only

As a poet who'd be better off a painter.
But this morning, later, I see all you took up
And moved with, while so many around you settled....

Most people stay put, or leave only where they came from,
Then settle. Not you; not me...Is the need to always go
A holy ambition or just a frightened turning

From the stillness, the staying? Are we better off
Staying in our rooms, cities, countries,
Or better incessantly *off* somewhere

And *out* in the weather of a relentless going?
Some argue for *balance* but we know
This is just the algebraic mind thinking,

Leaving us still to the unbalanced, extreme
Motions of living....There is no balance.
Why not say it? Why not say I was wrong

To so underestimate you.
Miss Bishop: Must we have
Our hopes and must we

Live them too?

WE SHOULD NOT LET MUNICH SLIP AWAY

There was rain which soon turned
To snow and no place we had in mind
We wanted to go so we stayed in bed

And made love all afternoon....
As the lamps lit the street
We got up from each other

Because there was money to be made
Because we did not grow our own food,
Because someone else owned that place;

So we got dressed for the club where
We went to play the music, where the people
From the offices spilled in from their day,

And you said we should go to Munich soon,
That we should not let Munich slip away—
That the work, the money was better there,

That things were not getting better for us here,
And that you had some money, some money
You'd not told me about—money squirrelled away.

All my life it's been a question:
Whether to go or to stay.
I woke up violent with fear one morning,

I woke up violent with hope one morning,
I picked up this horn one morning,
And it played me until I was away.

We are working wrong, and we know it,
And we do not know what to do about it.
We hoist our drinks—To yr health!—up to it

In order to escape, however briefly and bio-
Chemically, from it, but our problems,
As our mothers warned us (and Shelley

Himself chimed in with Do Not Go to Lethe!),
Are still there when we come down but, we feel,
Would have lingered otherwise like the unconscious

—No matter how much yoga or yogurt we subjected
Them to—so we say Fuck It and Let It, as they say,
Rip....We do savor our little holidays, before it

Is time to get back to it. We talk fairly
Non-stop about it; we sit in utter silence
And let the thousand splendid and sordid archetypes

Of our under-mind play around with it; we try
To stare it straight in the face or through charm
Cozy up to it, disarm it, or through brutish will

Show it we have the pluck, the drive needed
To blast right through it (running it straight
Up the middle is one of our favorite plays,

Though we prefer of course when possible
The evasive—Attaboy!—end-run), but more often than not
We end up collapsing into bed at blistered, crazed,

And pissed-off end of day beaten—veritably, lo I say
Unto you—into submission by it.
Mouthing our late-night agnostic prayers we beg

To be delivered from it before we get up next morning
And have to do it—Lord I do not think I can do it!—
All over again. Our children see it, fear it,

And begin, already, to move away from it. We saw it
In our parents and turned, in gloom,
Stuck out our fingers and hitchhiked away from it,

But the children's crusade, it is but a moment
—And the economy took a dive—and we were soon
Back, our faces shoved—Jesus Christ!—

Into the very crack of it. Thinking it
Was impossible to see it because we are *in it*
We then went at our brains with hallucinogens

Meant to dislodge, dissemble, and then—such
Was our violent hope!—recreate it, and out of this
Grew something resembling a culture (as opposed to,

Say, a market) which we took, for a moment, to be it,
But nothing, nay nothing I say unto you—not even It—
Can be made to stick in this world, in time, so in time

And to the market to which all hungers return, we turned
And, in sorrow and stupification, we got on with it....
We decided then to shove it and, as Mr. Creeley advised,

We bought huge fucking cars to drive our way, at least,
Narratively through it, and with car payments in tow
We began suddenly to respond to want ads promising us

More money if we would but do it, nudging us
Nine-to-fivewards towards that epiphany which intones,
In essence, "What the hell! *Stay with it!*"

We stare now at the Republican Party as if it were a cobra
About to strike us (It is!), but we are too hypnotized
—Such is its lurid charm, having captured the financial

And therein the political life of the nation—to do anything
About it, and the Democrats continue to devolve
As feckless shits held together by an ever-creaking

And cracking coalition of cobra-watching whiners....
O it ain't over till it's over, ain't completely broke
Until it's broken—and with this we wed, the marriage

Of citizen to country stuffed, the enstupidization
Of America continuing unabated at a terrifying rate.
Sometimes we do ponder various

Turnings-back or goings-forward such as moving
To a small farm outside the city where we might,
In consort with the beauty and the cruelty of

The Seasons, make our peace with it, but we do not
Do it because we sense for us (even for the farmers
Now?) this is not, nay not it at all.

Gary Snyder, for one, counsels us to Not Move, to
Stay Put, to commit to the cosmic fact that
All-Politics-Are-Local—and how we miss fatherly

Tip O'Neill, his great white hair always a fine shock!—
But the country (and with it our central nervous systems)
Have long since been on the wires and are part of

The National now, where our electric, our blood runs....
And blood, Lord, Lord Blood, how it does run.
We are tired of getting screwed and old enough now

To see our complicity in it—each a city in sorrow,
A suburb driving by in depression, a vast country
In muddled but now more-than-momentary mania—

And though we often consider the solace or at least
The novelty that might be gotten by going off
To some foreign country, where is that country

Foreign enough? Eastern Europe, with long lines?
Hope there now, and with hope of course violence....
We loathe those who live off inherited money

Whose job is only, it would seem, to buy their way
Through it, and we chastise ourselves for such petty
Ressentiments and look to see whether it's Capitalism

Or Socialism or some other distribution system
Which somehow caused it. And like those who came
Lo before us we grow old in a vale of tears

And horseshit, sore in the joints suddenly, ready
Almost—Death, stay thy phantoms!—for something
Final, some gasping closure to at least shape it.

We are lost in the middle way yet calling it
A "dark forest" does not really in any useful way
Locate us within it. Even when we are together,

Perhaps especially then, we are saddened to see
How little help we are, finally, to each other,
And this, more than anything, shoves us

Right up against it. We're nervous, impaled....
It might be we are suffering no more
Than our own self-consciousness and too much

Time to diddle it, too much affluence to forget it....
Leslie Howard in *The Petrified Forest* deftly called it
"Neurosis," a species of hellish payback for the spoiling

Of nature, and Robinson Jeffers certainly had it
Right about our vanity, our excessive preoccupation
With our own kind to the utter exclusion

Of the majesty—Say it, the kingdom!—broiling everywhere
All about us, if often to the side of us—our role perhaps only,
In some kind of impossible humility, to repair it....

And though we have done as Jeffers advised: We have
Leaned against the silent rock and felt its divinity, *shared*
In its nature, we most times staggered away

With Sartre's alienated—No, say *nauseated*—response
To the absurd tree where we sat watching, writhing,
Being with it, but came away finally only with our

Distance from it, out of it, unable
To commune because tricked out
By the mind's ability to imagine itself,

Come back over itself, and slip—with hardly
A moment's notice—out of all of it....And then there's
Always—and this we know best—the body.

We're fucked. We know it. Our only hope,
I think, is to find and do some decent work,
To give some repair as we go, we go hurling through it.

TOAST

To memory, that enormous bowl of water.
To what we imagined, what sent us off.
To that pitcher which poured us.

To water and to what we drink now
Which brings us back
As though we were water to each other.

HANS READING, HANS SMOKING

My mother, poised around behavior, would say
You are sitting there reading and smoking, Hans,
And this would describe for her, to her utter

Satisfaction, what it is you are doing.
Knowing you I guess you are stationed there
In grief, reverie, worry—your car broken

Down, the mechanic wanting money, and you without,
For the moment, what it takes—and you thinking
Of love lost as you read that impossible book

Your father last gave you....I see you smoking
And as an addict myself I know this is something
You are barely doing....The habit smokes itself

And you, you are turning the page where the woman
From New Orleans, like your woman, goes to Manhattan.
I suppose my mother, in her mania, could never afford

To think there was anything hovering around, anything
Behind behavior. Unable to sit, to go into that sorrow
Where what failed to happen presses against what did,

She would get up, go out looking for "Something
Different," do anything to keep moving, behaving...
Going. But you, Hans, you are a sitter, and I know

You will not be getting up until you have put this time
Behind you. And so your friends pass by waiting,
Wanting to know what you will come up with when you rise

From your stationary chair, our Hans reading and smoking.

MY PONY

Coming back to you, my pony, whom I had to leave
To make money, I proffer up the dire smidgen,
The torn truth I managed to lug back with me,

Along with the big bucks: World is made of bologna.
Like the pressed woods of my ascetic bookcase,
Like the traffic jam full of air conditioning

And grieving music, world is pressed together
As if by impossibility, my pony, as by poetry....
How long I have loved thee to see you now grown old

Though still able—under all this weight—
To put your foot to the far off, the going....
Carry me now, my pony. Carry us to where we buried

Those Clydesdales who once in soggy spring,
In early morning, plowed those furrows which fed us
Before I could no longer afford the farm.

I think we laid them down, me scrounging money
For the backhoe, over there in the west field.
I think we should go over now to the west field....

And the cats who used to run with us back
In the olde days: Sartre, Huck, and the others—
None lived to see fourteen, though all stayed relatively

Long for cat lives—blessings to them now, my pony;
Blessings to them who used to run and sit with us!
And will I ever get to hold my father as he dies

And will he release me then from the fear of dying?
Not likely. Probably not, my pony.
Probably much more muling through this membrane

Which passes so quickly, which stuns me and makes me
Wonder how much longer we've both got here to ride....
Ride on while we're here, my pony, and next spring

I'll bring Virginia, whom I've left back in the city.
I'll bring her to you for her safekeeping.
She needs the hurl and arc these fields have put in us,

Out looking; she needs the kind of joking past grieving
We've come to together, thrown through the pressed world
Where I went off to earn being hers and yours, your Liam.

NOTE ABOUT THE AUTHOR

Born in 1949 in Washington, D.C., Liam Rector's first book of poems was *The Sorrow of Architecture*, and he edited *The Day I Was Older: On the Poetry of Donald Hall.* He has received fellowships in poetry from the Guggenheim Foundation and the National Endowment for the Arts, and has administered literary programs at the Folger Shakespeare Library, the Academy of American Poets, Associated Writing Programs, and elsewhere. He has taught at a number of colleges and universities and is currently the director of the Writing Seminars at Bennington College in Vermont. He took graduate degrees from the Writing Seminars at Johns Hopkins and the Kennedy School of Government at Harvard, and he now resides in Massachusetts.